GOA kids | GOATS OF ANARCHY

PINEY
THE GOAT NANNY

Brimming with creative inspiration, how-to projects, and useful information to enrich your everyday life, Quarto Knows is a favorite destination for those pursuing their interests and passions. Visit our site and dig deeper with our books into your area of interest: Quarto Creates, Quarto Cooks, Quarto Homes, Quarto Lives, Quarto Drives, Quarto Explores, Quarto Gifts, or Quarto Kids.

Inspiring | Educating | Creating | Entertaining

First Published in 2018 by Walter Foster Jr., an imprint of The Quarto Group.
6 Orchard Road, Suite 100, Lake Forest, CA 92630, USA.
T (949) 380-7510 **F** (949) 380-7575 **www.QuartoKnows.com**

Walter Foster Jr. titles are also available at discount for retail, wholesale, promotional, and bulk purchase. For details, contact the Special Sales Manager by email at specialsales@quarto.com or by mail at The Quarto Group, Attn: Special Sales Manager, 401 Second Avenue North, Suite 310, Minneapolis, MN 55401 USA.

ISBN: 978-1-63322-332-5

Content development by Saskia Lacey
Illustrated by Jill Howarth

Printed in China
10 9 8 7 6 5 4 3 2 1

GOA *kids* | GOATS OF ANARCHY

PINEY
THE GOAT NANNY

By **LEANNE LAURICELLA** with *Saskia Lacey*

Illustrated by **JILL HOWARTH**

This is the story of a piglet named Piney.

Piney was adopted in the summer, when
the skies were their bluest, and the weather
was perfect for sprawling in the cool grass.

When he was young, Piney was small, striped, and round.
He could almost be mistaken for a watermelon!

The little pig spent his days splashing in the sun and his nights
bundled up in bed. He was happy in his new home.

Piney was curious about the other animals on the farm. There were
chickens, goats, a pony, and a donkey. Everyone looked so busy!

Piney's mom said that everyone on the farm had a job. The chickens ate the bugs and the goats chomped up the weeds.

The pony was in charge of eating the grass. He kept it nice and short.

The donkey's job was to chase the pony around. He helped the pony exercise after eating all the grass!

Piney wanted his own job. But what could he do around the house?

The pig tried helping in the kitchen, but his mom said, "No, Piney!"

Then, Piney tried to help clean, but his mom didn't let him do that either.

She told Piney that one day he would have a job, but for now, he should just enjoy being a piglet!

Months passed, and Piney grew bigger.
He even lost his cute watermelon stripes!

One afternoon, he woke to find a baby goat nearby. The little goat was crying softly.

Piney scooted closer to the goat. The crying softened. He moved even closer, curling up right next to the baby goat. The crying stopped completely.

The little goat's name was Prospect. Over the next few weeks, Prospect began to feel better and Piney kept him company.

Piney snuggled with Prospect, keeping him warm by the fire. He taught the little goat how to eat hay and drink water from a bowl.

Prospect was tiny but tough. With Piney's help, he grew feisty and strong.

One day, their mom said it was time for Prospect to move outside and live with the other goats.

Together, Piney and his mom watched the little goat join the others and begin to play.

Piney shuffled back to the fire. He wished he were a goat! Piney wanted to sleep outside with Prospect.

But he got a happy surprise when he woke from his nap. Two baby goats! One was a boy named Chibs and the other was a girl named Lyla.

Chibs had something wrong with his legs. They were all curled up and looked funny. Lyla only had three legs.

The baby goats cried and Piney moved closer. They cried again and he snuggled up next to them. After a few moments, the crying stopped.

Piney taught the little goats everything. He helped Chibs as his legs slowly straightened. He taught Lyla how to walk on only three legs! Soon, she was just as fast as the other goats.

Before long, it was time for Chibs and Lyla to live with the animals outside. Again, Piney watched as the two little goats left and joined the others.

This time, Piney didn't feel sad—he felt proud. He realized that THIS was his job. He took care of baby goats! He comforted them and taught them how to be strong.

Piney had the most important job of all—he was a goat nanny!

Piney couldn't wait to take his nap. He hoped that when he woke there would be another baby goat to care for. He fell asleep with a big smile across his snout.

When Piney woke from his nap, he saw a baby goat named Angel. She was missing her two back legs and looked very nervous. Piney snuggled close to Angel. He nudged her with his snout and said, "Don't worry little goat, I'll take care of you."

The End

PINEY
THE GOAT NANNY

The True Story

Hi, I'm Leanne Lauricella. People also call me "Goat Mama" because I rescue baby goats. I have a farm called Goats of Anarchy in New Jersey, where I care for more than 50 goats. Plus, we also take care of 2 lambs, 2 pigs, 6 dogs, chickens, a miniature horse, and a miniature donkey. We have a very full house!

Leanne

This is Piney. As a piglet, he looked like a little brown watermelon, stripes and all! When I first met him, he weighed about 7 pounds.

Now that he's grown up, he doesn't have stripes anymore. And he's big! Piney weighs about 100 pounds.

As a piglet, Piney's favorite treat was a spoonful of peanut butter. Now he loves eating sunflower seeds. We throw a handful of seeds into a kiddie pool and he goes after them for hours, just like he is bobbing for apples!

As Piney was getting adjusted to life on the farm, he wasn't quite sure where he belonged. He wanted a job just like everyone else on the farm! I used to tell him to just enjoy being a piglet and play. But he was determined to find his place.

Then one day I noticed how much he liked to snuggle with some of the baby goats. He was so good at comforting them, and they loved him too! Piney was a perfect goat nanny.

He kept his baby goats warm by the fire during nap time. He taught them how to eat and drink and take care of themselves. He even taught some of them how to walk.

Piney and Angel

Piney, Chibs, and Lyla

Chibs and Lyla

Piney lived inside the house for the first year of his life, taking care of all the baby goats. Then one day I heard about another piglet who needed help. I brought him home and we called him Winston.

Winston was tiny, and he thought Piney was his mom at first. Now Winston is even bigger than Piney! But they are still best friends and live together in the barn with the goats.

Piney still takes care of baby goats and helps them get used to life on the farm. He is the best goat nanny ever!

Piney and Winston